N

Life in Guatemala   1942

I was 5 years old when my life changed! Where were all the servants that always worked at our house?   At least Laya and Lena were there, I really liked them, Lena was our cook and Laya took care of the rooms upstairs and there was Tura of course. He was our butler, but he made it his special responsibility to take care of us and do things for us. We all loved Tura! But all the other servants were GONE! What happened? Mommy told us later that she had to tell them that she would not be able to pay their salaries anymore; they could stay with us to live but would have to look for work elsewhere. But dear Lena, Laya and Tura stayed with us. Then my Pappy was in jail!   Why was that?

He was the director of the big German Bank in Guatemala.   I remember my Mother going to the jail to take food for him every day. Of course Tura went with her. Later Mommy told us that all the German men were taken in and that they were going to take them to a Concentration camp in the US. I could not understand all these things and a World War didn't mean anything to me. That was far away and not here where we lived.

Since Maria our vegetable lady, didn't come any more to bring us all the vegetables and fruits that Mother wanted every week, Mommy decided to go to the market herself. That brought on a big discussion with Lena, she did not want my mother to go, she would go.

But Mother decided that she would go and I volunteered to go with her. So, off we went with the huge basked in our car. What a sight I saw, as we went down the few stairs to the Central Market. A symphony of colors! I saw all these ladies on the floor with their variety of fruits and vegetables in big baskets. All sorts of beautiful flowers. They had the most colorful embroidered blouses on. I thought it was amazing that so much color could be in one place!

We were not there for a minute and the huge basket was taken from me, I was glad, it was really heavy and this lady said that she was going to carry our basket. So we were taken over by Maria, this is not "our" Maria but another one; I guess there are a lot of "Marias' in this place.
So now we belonged to Maria and she would take over every week that we went to the market. She would carry this big basket all full of things we bought to our car on her head!

Pappy was taken to the US to a concentration camp with all the other German men, and we all felt lost! Who would do the drilling that we had every Saturday? Pappy would inspect our bed room and closets and everything had to be in perfect order, I mean military order! If we passed inspection, we would get our allowance. Now here Fred, my older brother, had a hard time! Just at the last minute he would run up the stairs to try to take care of his room. I did not have any trouble, because my older sister Rosie took care of our room. I never did it well enough for her. She sure mothered me and I didn't mind at all... Since I did not do anything well enough for her, she made our beds and fixed my closet all perfect, it always passed inspection and I thought it was just great. I sure love my sister Rosie! There was never any trouble with Eric, our other brother; he was the quiet one and no trouble with keeping his room orderly. Eric was the closest to me in age and we played a lot together.

We played cars in the sandbox and went swimming together in our big pool, climbed the trees. I was a regular tomboy! Eric would hear these series on the radio, it was called "El Zorro", and afterwards, he would tell me all about it. We would sit in a corner in our play room and he would tell me the story. It was always very exciting!

Mommy told us that things would not be as they were before; we would have to adjust to some changes. We had a big house and Tura would help with the cleaning, but we would have to do our part too. There were also the big garden, the swimming pool and tennis court. Tura did get a young boy to help him with the garden, but he felt in charge. I remember going with our mother with the car and waiting in long lines to get some gas. People would get frustrated many times and start blowing their horns. What a dumb thing to do! Mommy did manage to take us to the lake close by, once in a while. That was a treat! Dear Mommy, always trying to make things special for us even when at that time, it was difficult for her.

We always had a ball when we drove to the lake, which was close by, because our car was a Lincoln, twelve cylinders and it was exactly the same as the wife of the president's car. He had a property there too and when we came close to the curve where the big gate was, Fred would blow the horn and all the security men came running to open the gate for us and we just passed them and waved. It was always a game for us! Before all this happened, we went to the lake a lot. My brother Fred even had a little motor boat there.

We did have our cousins at home often,

since we had the big garden, we had lots of room to play and we loved our cousins.

I did miss my Pappy; I remember the times we drove to the different farms my Pappy had to supervise. The farms were big coffee farms that the company owned. That was always a lot of fun. As we approached the farm, we could see the entrance road with all the little white houses, where the workers lived, all lined up and the huge palm trees. It must have been a great occasion when we arrived, because we could hear the workers calling "alli viene el patron" that means here comes the boss. The women and children would line up on the road and wave. Mommy never forgot to take some goodies for the workers there, specially the children. We were greeted by the manager of the farm with a big glass of lemonade at the farm house. A beautiful wooden house with a huge deck all around it. We were allowed to ride the horses. Sometimes that was scary for me, because the horses did all right going, but coming back to the barn, nothing stopped them they would run without stopping. We had to bend down to avoid getting hit by the branches of the trees.

When Pappy still was with us, he and Mommy would go out at night. That was party time for us kids! We invited the cousins for a sleep over and we had the best pillow wars in the big family room upstairs. The family room was connected with the wide hallway to the bedrooms and that made a perfect place to stage our pillow throwing wars. Then we would slide down the big mahogany banister of the staircase. Laya scolded us, but we knew she would never tell our parents. She would come with a rag to be sure that everything was as shiny as it was before.

Christmas was always a big occasion. We were not allowed to see the decoration of the big Christmas tree in the living room until Christmas Eve. It was all very exciting and secretive. We were able to decorate our own tree in the play room, but the living room was out of limits, until we were summoned in with a bell on Christmas Eve.

What a special treat, when we finally were able to see the beautifully decorated big tree, the big table under it, with the manger scene on it. The manger scene had a lot of sheep and trees and little lakes, made with little mirrors with ducks on it and of course the stable with Mary, Joseph and little Baby Jesus in a crib with hay in it. Christmas music was playing, it was all very festive. The presents were not under the tree but on tables on one side. We had the Christmas dinner on Christmas Eve and were allowed to stay up till midnight when all the firecrackers started. Boy was that a noise! Lots of smoke all over and the dogs just hated it! But we thought it was just great!

Who would help Mommy decorate the tree? Now that Pappy was gone. Who would read the Christmas Story! Of course Tura helped Mommy decorate the tree! We did go to choose and buy the tree, it was smaller than usual and we only bought one tree, but that was OK with us. So Christmas turned out to be wonderful after all.

Our great uncle Richard helped Mommy a lot in these difficult days for her and also for us! Every Sunday, after going to

Church, we had lunch at his house. Tante Milly, his wife, always had a wonderful Sunday dinner and in the afternoon, it was play time with Uncle in the garden. We played bocce with a passion. Especially Uncle took it very seriously and we followed his example. On rainy days we would play "golf". Uncle opened all the connecting doors of the three bedrooms and off went the little golf ball hopefully into the small tray in the last bedroom. Tante Milly did not like our "sport" in the rooms but I guess she had no choice.

Tante Milly played the piano and she would sing with us, she had a beautiful voice.

We also had to change schools. All the German teachers of the German School were deported and the School was closed. Mommy told us later that she had a hard time getting us into another school, but finally we were accepted into a Catholic nun's school. Fred and Eric went to a Catholic boys school and Rosie and I to the nun's school. The only thing I did not like was that we had to wear a uniform with a long sleeved blouse and even wear it when it was so hot. The Mother Superior scared me. She was always so serious and she was so round and big. Too scary! So life went on, but we did miss Pappy!

Mommy seemed more worried also, although she never told us anything. Dear Mommy always trying to make the best of everything,

Changes   1944

Pappy still was in the US, he did not go to Germany, like so many of the men that were taken to the concentration camp. He did not want to go to Germany and it was allowed him to stay in the US. Pappy told us later that he was treated well. Things were getting tight for us too. Mommy told us that it would be better if we don't talk in German in the street; I thought that was real dumb. Mommy preferred for us to stay at home, when we got back from school, which was no problem, we had the big garden and our friends loved to come and also we had our cousins who were there most of the time. Tura, Lena and Laya continued to take care of us. Rosie and I walked to school which meant that I had to wait so long coming home, because Rosie had to finish the story she was telling her friend Concha and I thought it took forever! It was fun when it rained, because I would step into the puddles and splash all over. Mommy was always glad when we got home. She worried about us.

Fred was going to the university now. He went on the city bus, but one day Fred didn't come home! That was scary! Mom was really worried. What had happened? I will let Fred tell the story: "We were coming out of the university in the afternoon, when we were surrounded by soldiers with guns. They told us to make a line, and a man started shouting at us that we had to serve our country. There was a Revolution. We were given a gun and taken to a secluded place and told that we should shoot anything that moved. We were told how to use the guns and left there. We hid under a bush and waited. It was getting dark. Suddenly we heard foot steps! We did not know what to do and did not see anything. One of my friends, Eddie, said he had to go the bath room. Of course we all told him to be quiet and hold it. Foot steps were getting closer! We tried to be real quiet, Eddie kept telling us that he had to go, shh... be quiet! The footsteps kept coming closer and closer, should we shoot? Finally, Eddie had the courage to come out a little bit and here he saw the enemy! It was a cow! We were so relieved and Eddie was too! Early the next morning, we were picked up. They took away the arms and told us to go home. So we all walked home."

Boy, we were so happy to see Fred and Mommy was too.

Mommy kept going to the lawyer's office, we did not know why. She really looked worried until finally she told us that the government was trying to confiscate our home as they had done to so many German families that were gone, many farms were confiscated too, so was the bank my father had managed and also a property that Pappy owned. Friends and even Uncle Richard were telling Mommy to get out of the house and at least try to save some of the furniture, but she refused and said that this was her home and she did not know where to go. One day she got a summons telling her that on that date they were coming to take over the property. Boy, were we scared! That day, Mommy told us to stay in the house and she went out to the gate alone. Even Tura was not allowed to go with Mommy. She was very serious about that. We all stood at the window looking out to see what was happening. Lena and Laya were there with worried faces. I think it took forever for Mommy to come back in. She finally did and just told us "They are not going to bother us again" then she went upstairs and closed the door of her room. Many years later she told us what she had done.

When she got to the gate, the men, about six men, gave her an official paper and told her that they came to take over the house. Mommy looked at the paper and told them that this was her home, she did not have any place to go and the only way they would be able to get her out of her home was to shoot her, her 4 children and her old mother and that she was going to call the press to be there too. That was the end of that and we were never bothered again.

Sweet, loving Mommy, she sure was a courageous lady. She just told us that when anybody wanted to harm her children, she would turn into a lioness.

That brings me to our Grandmother, Oma. She lived with us all the time, ever since I can remember. Our grandfather died very young and Oma lived with us ever since. Oma had two sisters, one was our Tante Milly and the other Tante Clara. Then there was Uncle Henry. What a character he was. He was a lot of fun to be with, always happy and full of life and jokes.

When we visited Tante Clara, the maids made it their business to feed us. It never ended! Our special treat was her parrot. He would talk all the time. He would call the maids by name and tell them that it was time to go to bed or to eat. He even made all the movements as if he was brushing his teeth. Lorito was so much fun!

Oma was the more serious of the three

sisters, but we were allowed to lay down on her bed, if we were nice and quiet, that was a treat for me.

1947

There is great excitement in our house now! Pappy is coming home and everybody is busy. Tura and the boy in the garden, Lena preparing food and Laya and us kids cleaning and polishing everything in the house. I did miss my Pappy, even the Saturday drills in our rooms. I am 10 years old now and I know now what the War was all about and how it affected so many people, including us. Our house in Germany was completely destroyed, we did not even know if our aunt and cousin Reni had survived the attack on Dresden, where they lived in our house. Yes wars are cruel, but now Pappy was coming home and everything was going to be all right as it was before! Of course, that was not the case, Pappy came home and now our parents had to figure out what to do next. The bank was confiscated, Pappy's money was gone, the company where Pappy worked was closed. We moved to the downstairs, since the house is so big, no problem. Rosie and I slept in the play room, our parents in the sport room and the boys in the carpentry room. There was one bathroom that we all had to share. The upstairs was converted into a Bed and Breakfast place. We had many interesting people stay in our Bed and Breakfast.

Mommy had a lot of work with it while Pappy tried to get his life together again. Dear faithful Lena, Laya and Tura never left us. I remember that we had to help too, when we were not in school or doing homework. I sometimes had to take the breakfast to a man upstairs. He did not want to be disturbed and called when he wanted his breakfast. He was kind to me and sometimes he talked to me, but other times he just motioned to leave the tray there. Later I found out that he is a writer and wrote his book while he was at our house.

Much later he sent his book to my mother and dedicated it to her, with a
Note of Thanks! I wish now I knew the name of the author!

1948
Pappy opened a grocery store with a man
from Spain. It was a big grocery store
and they even delivered groceries to the
homes. Mommy did not have the Bed and
Breakfast any more, but they rented out
part of the house to a family, so we still
lived downstairs.

We went to help in the store when we
were on vacation. We helped decorate
and fill baskets that were delivered to
faithful clients, during the Christmas
Season. It was kind of fun to help there.
It was a busy place. Pappy hired some
young men that had just come back from
Germany. There was one young man
there, his name was Walter. He was so
serious and always working hard. He
came to work at Pappy's store in 1949.
Pappy sure liked him and soon this
Walter became Pappy's right hand. We
saw Walter in Church too.

The youth group in Church was formed
and many Sundays in the afternoon the
young people came to our house to play
and have fun. Mommy always had
goodies prepared for us.

I remember one time when Rosie touched my arm and winked at me and asked me "Hey how about Walter, do you like him?" "No way, he is so serious and so hard working, just like Pappy!" I said. Who would have thought that he would play such an important part in my life later! Life went on, not as I had imagined that everything was going to be like it was before Pappy left, but life was good.

I was enrolled at the American School and that was so wonderful, I just loved the change. Lena was getting older now, she did have her niece helping her, but she was getting tired and decided to go back to her people. Laya went also to take care of her. That was a sad day for us. They did come to visit us once in a while.

New mission in Guatemala

The first missionary for Guatemala came in 1948. While Pappy was in the concentration camp in the States,

Lutheran Pastors from the Missouri Synod came to visit him. So when Pappy came back to Guatemala, he asked the Synod to send a Missionary to Guatemala. Our first missionary, Pastor Robert Gussick and his dear wife Ruth with Baby Carol came to Guatemala. Pappy and Mommy went to the airport to pick them up. They sure looked tired and so was the Baby. Ruth tried to get the baby bottle out of her bag for Baby Carol and dropped it. The glass bottle went to pieces and dear Ruth started to cry and so did Baby Carol. As always Pappy took care of everything and Baby and mother were taken to the place where they were staying. Another baby bottle was provided. I bet they had a good nights sleep! We had the first service at my Parents house, what a special occasion.

I sure missed my brother Fred. He went to a University in Ontario Canada. He used to tease me a lot, but he was good to me. Fred was 10 years older than I. I loved it when he played the piano. My favorite was the Polonaise of Chopin. Fred had the gift of music. I had to take piano lessons also, but I never made it to anything special.

1950

This was a sad year for me. Rosie was sent to college in the States, I hated to see her go. Rosie was only 18 years old and here she went to a completely new experience in a different country and different way of life. I sure missed her! Rosie survived all this new happenings in College and even met her husband there.

When Rosie and Jerry wanted to get married in 1955 she came home, of course the wedding had to be at our house. Pappy would not have it any other way! First thing we had to do was rename our dog. His name was Jerry and now it had to be Teddy. I'm glad Teddy understood the change. Teddy was not a very friendly dog to strangers, but he was very loving to us. When Jerry came to our house, Teddy accepted him right away, I think he figured his name sake must be all right. Who would have thought that this nice quiet man would much later become the head of the landing operations for the space shuttle! He also worked with the X15 plane.

Rosie and Jerry's wedding was lovely, I was the maid of honor and who do you think was the best man? Serious Walter! I was madly in love with him then and I guess he convinced me that he could be fun too. Walter played the accordion for our youth group parties and he and I sure made good partners for our square dancing. God brought us together and I am very thankful for that.

Eric went to college in the States, I sure missed him also! Later he went to Germany to study medicine. It was a long study. He stayed there for years although he came home for my Birthday once. That was so special for me. He made an extra special effort to come home for my Birthday! After his studies, Eric came back to Guatemala to work among the poor. Dear quiet Eric, it was not until his death that we found out how much he did for them and how much he was loved and admired among them. I remember that sometimes he brought live chickens home. They were given to him as a payment.

Pappy sold the grocery store and we were glad about that, it was getting difficult working with his partner who had so different values.

Pappy started with the coffee business again something he always loved and was also a consultant with the new generation of the German coffee business men that had come to Guatemala before the war.

Christmas still was very special in our house, even though we missed Fred, Rosie and Eric. The traditional big Christmas tree went up, the many cookies were baked and my beloved angels with their musical instruments were put out on the "heavenly ladder" like I called it.

Tura still helped with the decoration of the tree. Mommy and Pappy had many Christmas parties with all the friends and family, one of the very special ones was the first Sunday in Advent. Mommy fixed the huge formal dinning room table with all the Christmas goodies and decorations. Their Christmas parties were special and people loved to come to them. Many times, much later when Mommy and Pappy were not here anymore, people would mention them to me.

We had the day dining room where we ate every day. The formal dining room was just for special occasions.

Walter and I got engaged on Christmas 1955. Back then the groom had to ask the parents for the hand of their daughter. It was a very formal thing and we celebrated with champagne although my parents already knew that we wanted to get married. . We were married June 2, 1956!!!

Before I go on with our life together, Walter has to tell his story, how he had to leave Guatemala and how he got back.

Walter's story   1943

I was 12 years old when my Father was taken right from his office in Guatemala to prison and then on to a concentration camp in Camp Landing in Florida. Like all the German men were taken.

Mother and I were worried, what would happen to us without Father being there? I felt responsible for my Mother and my sister Inge. Father told me, when he left "Now you are the man in the house" but... what could I do? There were a lot of telephone calls among the wives that had been left behind. The men were shipped to Germany with all the other men as prisoners of war exchange.

Father had left his trucks with a friend. He had a transportation business of all the coffee and other products that were shipped to Germany. Luckily we had our own house that my parents built. Finally we got word from the German Embassy that the German government was sending a Spanish neutral ship to pick up all the wives and children. What a relief!

We had to pack in a hurry and we did leave a lot of things behind. A Guatemalan family moved into our house and said that they would take care of it for us.. Mother took some clothes for

Father and also something to eat. She also took her coffee and other things.   We knew we were going into a war zone. Who knows how it was going to be. We were taken to the port in the Atlantic side of   Guatemala   by   train,   another adventure! Finally we were able to go on the ship and I was all excited to be in a big ship going to Germany.

Inge, my sister, was excited too.   Only Mother had her misgivings.
We were given a room for ourselves, Mother and Inge slept in one bed and I had the bunk bed all to myself.

Many families that we knew were on board. There was a lot of talking and sharing between the mothers.

Getting to the Island of Trinidad, we were guided by a tuck boat to a British Navy Base.   We had a lot to see!   British marines came on board and to our dismay they confiscated all the things that the wives had so carefully packed for their men. Mother was not going to give up her coffee beans, so she poured honey all over the coffee and they didn't take that messy stuff. Later Mother washed her coffee beans and was all happy that she saved her treasure. Leaving the port was another exciting adventure, there were sirens going on and the ship just started without being tucked away. Later the captain told us that the British wanted to guide us all the way to Germany. That would be dangerous because we could be attacked by the German submarines, because of the British ships. So mines or not, the captain just took off hoping he would not hit a mine. The ship went to a port in Portugal and from there we were picked up by the German government and taken to Germany by train.

We were always wondering why all the windows were blackened while we were traveling through France and Germany. It was to avoid being bombarded.

Into war torn Germany   1943

Finally we were at our destination, Stuttgart. What a shock, our eyes were opened to what war is really about. We saw all the coffins all lined up in a place, buildings destroyed, it was grueling. Father was not there to pick us up, we did not know what to do. Finally we saw our uncle who came to pick us up to go to St. Georgen, a little village right at the highest point in the Black Forest. Tante Berta was waiting for us and we were able to live with her on the second floor of her house, all during the war.

We were thankful that we were not in a big city, so we were not bombarded. But life got complicated, especially for Mother. Provisions were scarce we had to go by what was available. Most of the time we had potatoes for every meal, in the morning, at noon and at night. Many times not even that. At the beginning we got food stamps to get something, but that stopped soon. The good part is that we were able to visit our grandparents and uncle at the farm. That is where my father grew up.

My grandfather was a farmer, they had 9 children, but most of them had left the farm, so only my grandparents and one uncle were there. But we could get some of the produce they had planted. It was also a dairy farm, so we usually came back with milk and some cheese made right there. Many times Mother made a delicious soup out of browned flower and water with a little bit of salt. So we got along, you get inventive, when you have to. I made sandals out of old tires for summer. We did go to school, that was many times interrupted because of bomb alarms. I also had to join the "Jungvolk" that is like the boy scouts here. They made us do hard things to be able to get our reward. I had to run the track twice because I was not able to swim in the lake that much because it was so cold. I was not 15 years old yet, or I would have been drafted to the army. 15 years old kids were enlisted to serve! Once we heard a bomb fly by, not so far away from the house. It was a scary sound. It made a big hole not so far away.

Life went on and I am thankful to God for these hard times because we learned to be thankful for what you have and that even in hard times, God provides and is there with us. When possible, we went to

Church on Sundays. I also joined the brass choir, where I learned a lot about music. A brass choir is not a band. It is a group of brass instruments that play and sounds like a choir. I played the trumpet. We were in Germany during the worst time 1943 to 1949 when things got a little better. St. Georgen was invaded by the French troops. Those were dangerous times for us because the German forces tried to re-conquer the city and the French troops fought back and we were in the middle of the fighting. Five grenades exploded in our garden, our neighbor's house was hit but we were spared. God's protection!!

Since St Georgen, the town where we lived up in the mountains, had such a good climate, the French occupation troops had a camp for French children there and we were able to see all the goodies they got and we just had to look! But strangely enough, we looked much healthier than those children. Mother and I talked about going back to Guatemala, where we had our own house.

Going back to Guatemala   1949

This was quite a feat.   Getting permit papers even to leave Germany was a hassle, then getting papers for Mother, as German citizen, she was not permitted to land in so many countries.

No money, no passports!   We had to go to Paris to get passports.   When we left St. Georgen, we were very touched to see the whole brass choir and many friends at the train station to say good bye! We had tears in our eyes. My best friend Dieter gave me this Bible verse as a farewell : *"Being confident of this very thing, that He who has begun a good work in you will complete it until the day of Jesus Christ."* Philippians 1:6

When we were in Paris, we heard that the Italian shipping line that we were going to take was on strike.

Our uncle in Guatemala had sent the money, but it was not there at the Guatemalan Embassy.   We waited for 3 weeks to get the money and the kind man in the little hotel where we were, let us stay there without pay. There are kind people all over the world. Fortunately the Italian shipping company returned the money of our fares to the Guatemalan Embassy in Paris and so we were able to fly to Venezuela, the only country that accepted German citizens. Here comes the interesting adventure of our flight to Venezuela. From Paris to Reykjavik, Iceland, then on to Sidney, Canada, on to New York and finally to Venezuela. On all the places that we landed, we were not allowed to step outside of the airport. Here in Venezuela, we were stranded again! No money, fortunately the owner of the Hotel we stayed in, advanced the money to purchase my ticket.

I flew to Guatemala alone to find out about the money and when I got there I had forgotten all my Spanish! I was looked at suspiciously at the airport in Guatemala city, a Guatemalan passport and... no Spanish! I found out that Uncle had sent the money and finally two weeks later, mother and Inge were able to fly to Guatemala also.

My uncle Christian let us live in

Parramos with them on their farm. Now I had to find a job to be able to support my Mother and sister. Luckily I found out that Mr. Martin hired young German men that came back to Guatemala. I was hired by him and quickly became his right hand. I learned a lot with him and who would have thought that later he became my Father in Law! We had to get our house back also, the tenants were not very eager to get out of the house, but we finally got that straightened out also. In the meantime Mother and Inge lived at the farm in Parramos. Mother started to make her famous cookies to sell and became quite famous with them.

I met Heidi at the store where I worked with her father and also in Church, she was only 14 years old. She was just a little kid for me, and she definitely was not interested in me. I went to the youth group in church and started to play the organ for the services. I also started the choir, where Heidi and her brother also attended. Years went by and suddenly Heidi was a young lady and got very interesting to me! God works in special and mysterious ways."

Wedding Bells   1956

June 2, 1956. Now it is my (Heidi's) turn to tell the story: Our wedding day! At that time I thought it was the most wonderful day of my life, without knowing that later, there were going to be more wonderful days.   Pappy arranged for all the details of our wedding and reception and of course he always did a marvelous job. My dear Rosie came and also Eric for the special occasion. How I loved to see them again! Rosie bought my wedding dress in the States, so I didn't see my dress until a few days before the wedding!   That is real trust in my sister! We were going to go to Europe for our honeymoon but the first night we went to an old farm house in Guatemala, where the owner made wine.   The first night we were so tired from all the festivity that we just cuddled together and went to sleep. The next morning we went back to my parents home to see our presents and pack for the trip.

Our honeymoon!   We flew to Miami, FL

and here the trouble started! Have you ever met a new husband who had to spend the first night and day with his wife, washing her underwear and blouse? I felt like I wanted the earth to swallow me! It was here I found out that I was seriously allergic to sea food. The first dinner in Miami we ate sea food and I got seriously sick. Poor Walter, what a honeymoon! I did not know that I was allergic to sea food, because we never had it at home because my Mother is allergic to sea food also.

I think I was sick for three days! I just wanted to die! When I was feeling better, we drove a car all the way to New York where we embarked to Germany. This car belonged to a rich man who left his car and wanted it to be driven to his home in New York. I had the joy to be able to visit my brother Fred and his wife Jean who lived in Davies Island New York. We got to see our niece Sue. What a sweet little girl! She must have been three or five years old. It was so nice to be able to visit with them! Finally things went better from there. Walter ordered a car which we picked up in Ruedesheim,

Germany. It was an Opel Kapitan. We were very proud of our car.

Now off to visit the relatives in the Black Forest. And here comes Heidi's first experience of being a wife. I think Walter thought that all girls were born with the ability to do everything a wife is supposed to do. His first request was to wash and iron his suit. His suit!! I had never washed nor ironed anything at home. We were at Tante Liesel's home and I asked her to help me, but she had lost her husband during the war and she had no idea, nor experience with ironing men's clothes. I was brave and tackled the job. The baths were only on Saturdays. What a change from home! I think sometimes I was homesick, but most of the time we enjoyed the beautiful scenery and the love of all the relatives. Time went by so quickly and soon it was time to go home to Guatemala. We took our car with us, it was a freight ship that took a few passengers. We embarked in Bremerhafen. There, when the ship started to go by, a band played " "Nun Ade Du mein lieb Heimatland" : " Say good bye to your homeland" Somehow we had tears in our eyes.

The weather was not so good and many times the only ones in the dinning room were Walter and I. Many got seasick.

We disembarked in New York and drove all the way to Guatemala through Mexico. We had to put the car on a train crossing over to Guatemala in the highlands. Boy was it HOT. But we survived.

Back home, what a relief! My parent's home is so big that we could have a complete apartment with living room, bedrooms and kitchen with dining room all to ourselves. Dear Mommy and Walter's Mother had fixed it all so nice for us!

Here comes the challenge! I was supposed to be able to cook, bake and do all the things his mother did so well. Pride helped me and willingness to learn, but it was hard!

Speaking of other most wonderful times in our lives, there were a lot! The first one was the birth of our first son, Eric. What a beautiful and good Baby he was.

Eric is still such blessing for us! Eric was born July 7 l957.

Here comes another wonderful happening in our lives! Our second son, Gerhard, was born December 19, l958. Almost a Christmas present! Gerhard came with a bang and with a lot of excitement. There were many earthquakes at that time, everybody feared a big earthquake. The hospital had big tents put up in a vacant lot near by, just in case. A big earthquake did come, but about that, I will tell you later. For now, at the hospital I wanted to see where my Baby was at the nursery so that I could run and get him, just in case. I never did get to the nursery, on the way I got dizzy and almost fainted. A nurse just got me in time. I guess I had lost too much blood at the delivery. Gerhard was a happy, "go get it" Baby and child. We just loved him so much. We still do! When he learned to walk, he just closed his eyes and "here I come"! Get up and fall again.

Our boys were close in age and practically grew up as twins. Now having three boys in the family, father and two sons, my life was full of adventure. All three were very active and full of plans. We bought a boat before we had a house. I am sure our parents thought we were crazy. We camped in a tent at the big lake; that was before disposable diapers and ready-made baby food! Of course, our dogs, two dachshunds had to come too. Later, Walter built a house at the lake and that became easier for me. This lake is Atitlan Lake, a beautiful big lake surrounded by mountains and two volcanoes, really beautiful!

The caretaker's son at the lake became our "third son" The boys did everything together. Even before we drove to the house, the boys were calling him Teta, Teta! That was his nickname.

Life went on, the boys were ready for school and all the activities in school, as all parents know about.

1964 another milestone for us, I was expecting a Baby! I was hoping for a little girl, but God decided otherwise and little sweet Arnold was born. Arnold was the sweetest child I have ever known, sometimes I wonder if God sent us a little angel just for a time. Three years later Anika was born. Anika was all life and sure of herself. She was my Pappy's adoration. She could get away with everything with him, not at all, as we were brought up with Pappy. Not even our boys had all this attention and privileges that Anika had.

Tragedy! 1969

Life was good and everything was just right for me. But then... did you ever feel that life had to stop and that you did not want to go on anymore? Life just ended for me! How can anything like this happen? We were coming back from the lake, the road to the lake is very curvy, and Guatemala is very mountainous. There was a lot of fog. The boys were sitting in the back seat and the two little ones with me in the front. At that time, we did not even have seat belts in our car.

I do not remember much about the crash

because I lost consciousness.
I do remember being taken to a hospital in a little village near by.

I also saw my dear brother Eric who had driven all the way from the city to see how he could help. It was so good to see him. Then all is a blur, just when I was put in the helicopter that took us to the city, I heard our friend tell me "now you have to be real brave". I wondered why I had to be brave. But then I saw two little figures wrapped in white sheets, my life just ended right then and there! The only thing I remember about the trip on the helicopter was that I asked God to please let the helicopter fall down, just a little engine trouble and down we crash. Or maybe God could make my heart just stop. I really was sincere about my petition. But we did arrive at the airport in the city and I just remember all in a blur, me in a stretcher and a lot of people hugging me and telling me not to cry or to cry and I really didn't know what was going on. At the hospital we got attention right away. I remember telling the Dr. that my back hurts and he told me "Lady, that is the least of the troubles I have with you" That sure helps!

Later I found out that I had severe concussion, fearing that I would go blind, 5 ribs broken, two vertebrae broken and my foot completely smashed. Not a very good picture, I would say. The only light ray that I saw was that my sister Rosie came all the way from California to be with me. My Rosie was there and I felt a little light coming towards me. I never saw how I looked, but judging by the expression of the people that came to visit, I must have looked awful.

I was put into a body cast from where my arms start to where my legs begin and also the one leg from under the knee all the way down covering my foot. We stayed at the hospital for 1-1/2 months. Poor Walter had to stay there too. Thank God he was not hurt severely but, in Guatemala you are guilty till proven innocent and that took a while to straighten things out. This pick up truck that crashed with us must not have seen us because it was so very foggy. They must have been speeding too. So we even had a policeman in front of our door at the hospital till that was cleared. When I think about it now, I really feel sorry for Walter, all the attention and care was given to me, but what about him? He suffered too! He just took it all silently. Rosie was such a help and comfort to me. She also took care of our two boys Eric and Gerhard. I thank the Lord that they were not hurt!! They were in the back seat. Rosie went to our home with our two boys and took care of them, saw to it that they do their homework and tried to do things as normally as she could. Dear Rosie, I'll always be thankful to her.

We finally could go home, me and all my casts, and how life went on, I don't really know, but somehow God, in His incredible love and mercy, took this little peace of nothing, physically and spiritually and slowly made something of it. My Mommy was such a help and strength for me, how could I have done without her. She was such a source of strength and love. So was my sister Rosie, who took such good care of our boys and was always there for me. Pappy just stayed at the side, never said much. But Mommy told me later, that ever since the accident Pappy went slowly down hill. We never went to our little ones funeral because we were at the hospital, but Mommy told me that Pappy cried bitterly. When I think back, I also feel sorry for our two boys, I was in such a stupor that I really could not pay much attention to them. Now I feel sorry! I also feel sorry for Walter, all the attention and love went out to me, I don't think Walter got the support and attention that he should have gotten.

My dear friend Judith came several days a week to do exercise with me, I could hardly move my head. The casts came off after four months and then I lost all my balance! I had to wear a metal brace which I could take off for the night. Judith helped me so much to get back my balance and to move my head and all my limbs.

It was time for Rosie to go back home! I hated to see her go, but she had a family in the States too. Thank you Jerry for lending her to me!

Yes, God works in mysterious ways. I

can't imagine how He did it, but suddenly life became livable again for me. Family life became normal. Our dear boys and Walter survived a confused and absent mother and wife.

Two months later God gave me my best friend Jan, a missionary wife that came to Guatemala. Jan became such a special part of my life. I thank God for the time we had together. Later I will tell you how I had to say good bye to Jan. Very sad!

To get busy and not be able to think so much, I decided to open a vacation camp at Pappy's house with the big garden. All school friends of our boys came and I think all had a good time. We even had a Christmas play where we invited the parents. In Guatemala vacation time was from November to January. Our play was about the Drummer Boy, with music and all. We had some exciting things happen, once one of the boys decided to make a fire, we almost had a brush fire!! These boys sure were active! But I had a lot of fun with them and I kept busy.

Life with our boys, 1970

This year we went to Europe with our boys. We visited the aunts, who spoiled the boys with chocolate. Our Eric was 13 years old and Gerhard almost 12. We rented a car and I remember Eric traveling through the French Riviera, reading his books in the back seat! I do hope our boys will remember this trip as something special we did together.

Coming back home, life went on, schoolwork, school plays, birthday parties, going to the lake, activities in Church. We took in a boy from the street. Jorge was his name, he was a good boy. I remember that I used to go to the boys room when they were sleeping and give each one of my kids a kiss. The next day Jorge told me that I didn't give him a kiss. So the next many nights Jorge got a kiss too. Our boys got along fine with him too. They all slept in the same room. Poor Jorge had such a bad infection and I had to cure him. He didn't like the treatment at all. I had to give him antibiotics every 6 hours and at night, when he was asleep, it was a challenge to get him to swallow the pill, because he did not wake up easily! We only had Jorge during vacation time, during school our friend inscribed him in a Christian school. As an adult, Jorge came to visit us. I am so glad that he made it in life, he went to the States, got married and at that time they had a little daughter.

Walter started a brass choir in Church and our two boys each played the trombone. I was kind of proud.

Life gets busy with a family of boys and Walter had to travel through Central America and Venezuela, so, many times I had to cope alone and here I was the girl that didn't want to live, (remember after the accident?) God had made an active satisfied person, I don't know how! How did He do it??

Life with three boys can be exciting and fun. "All things work together for the good for those who love the Lord" The thing is, sometimes I didn't even know that I loved the Lord. One thing I know for sure! He loves me!!! My Lord Jesus even gave His life for me! That is true LOVE.

There are special milestones in each person's life and this year it was for us. Eric went to his first year in college in the US at Concordia College in Seward Nebraska. Here he was, never gone away from home, grew up in a different country and culture. I don't know who was more worried, the mother or the child!

He started in January mid-term in winter and he had never been any place in winter never had seen snow, not even had the right cloths for winter. Eddie, a dear friend from Kansas, was so helpful and helped us get the right clothing and even boots. I still think of Eddie's father, he was so helpful to us too! He gave Eric the boots. He was such a kind and nice man. I've learned that God provides in wonderful ways. To my big surprise, Eric did so well in college. Do you know what culture shock is? Well, Eric experienced it, when he worked at the cafeteria in college and saw how much food was thrown away. He told us once that he wanted to grab all this food and bread and send it to the poor people in Guatemala. Eric said he had wonderful friends and they helped him in so many ways, they also had fun with him, teasing him because of his different ways and accent. Then our Gerhard had to go to college, thankfully he could go to the university in Guatemala and we did not have to say good bye to him.

The only thing is, your children grow up and the mothers have a hard time realizing it. Gerhard did so well at the university and even graduated with a Masters degree in chemical engineering.

He went to the university with Walter's motorcycle every day and there were many nights, when I had to sing hymns, so as to keep calm and not despair too much, when he didn't get back in time. The University was far away and the traffic in Guatemala is a challenge. You can imagine, a young boy on a motorcycle! Once he had an accident. He was coming home, had the right of way where he was driving, and out comes a car right when he was passing that street. Gerhard crashed into the car and flew over it. Can you imagine!!! And he did not have a scratch on him. I don't know how he did it. The man was so nice as to take Gerhard home. The man knew he was at fault. He even offered to pay for damages.

The big earthquake   1976

Hard times to go through!!   Pappy died in 1975. With him, a special epoch in our lives went also, but we were glad that he did not have to go through the big earthquake that hit Guatemala. This was in 1976. What an experience that was! Have you ever felt as if something terrible is happening and it takes you a while to realize what it is? You hear a rumbling, like a train is coming full force, very noisy and then everything starts moving. It was 3 o'clock in the morning, we were in bed and it took us some time to realize that we have a big earthquake. Our house was a mess, the bookcases tumbled down, the glass door to the patio opened, the piano was in the middle of the living room and we were all dazed.

Walter and I went to the boys room and Eric was climbing out the window, we looked into Gerhard's room and he was sleeping!! I could not believe it, I thought he was hurt. We all rushed out of the house, and with all the aftershocks, we slept in our tent in the garden for more than a week. No water, no electricity! We even were afraid to get something out of the house, like cloths and get something to eat. Later we found out the destruction that this earthquake did. 34,000 people dead, I don't know how many houses destroyed. Big devastation and lots of people lost their homes. Many countries came to help, brought tents and food. Our boys and Walter also went to help where they could. In times of crisis, people do get together and try to help each other.

Other adventures with the boys

So, to more fun things: "Life with my three 'boys" Walter, and our sons Eric and Gerhard. Boys are fun to be with specially "my boys". The minute we got to the big lake, off we went with the boat. Walter bought an old motor boat that he fixed. Gerhard loved to spear fish, we all swam like fish and water skiing was a matter of course and our dogs the dachshunds, came along too. All this till the big winds came and we had to rush to get to where we put the boat out. This was not a ramp, just a sand slope. The strong winds were dangerous, I think many a time God sent some more angels to protect us. We never had a life west, never knew what that is till later, when we tried to use our kayak on a lake in the States and were warned by someone that we can only use the kayak with life vests, which we got later!

Then there was the time when the boys wanted to go around the lake with their "home made" kayak and the boat and got caught in the big wind! I don't know how they made it back. I did not go with them that time. They were going to paddle around the whole lake, of course the wind stopped this adventure fast.

There is a creek on our property in the

city, down in the ravine. When their friends came to visit, the boys would go down to the creek and to be able to get to the waterfall they had to pass the canyon holding on with their feet on one side and their hands on the other. It's good that I never saw that, they just told me when they got back to the house all muddy and filthy. Are all boys like these?

I wonder what they did when they rescued the little puppy they heard crying also in the ravine. We adopted the puppy and named him Robin. I will tell you about him later.

1983
Mommy got sick Nov. 1983 Dear Mommy who never complained about anything. It's scary when you feel that you can't breathe! Her lungs were giving out and so was her tired heart. She went in and out of the hospital several times. When I was with her at the hospital, I taught myself how to crochet, just to keep busy. My brother Eric and I took turns in sleeping with her every other night. I was not with her when she went home to her heavenly Father, Eric was and he

called me early in the morning. I was sad but also glad for her. What a funeral that was! Mommy sure had a lot of friends. I have never seen so many flowers. God granted her wish, she wanted to die at home and leave from her home.

When Mommy got sick she mentioned several times that she would like to be there when Gerhard would get married. I always told her "of course you still will be here to see your grandson getting married", but she didn't make it. Mommy died in April and Gerhard and Roxana got married in June.

Our boys grow up

June 1983 Gerhard is getting married to Roxana. What an adventurous wedding that was. The reception was going to be at our house. The boys and Walter put up a canopy in our patio, just in case it rains. The reception was in the evening. Well it did rain! Not in the evening, but at noon time. The canopy sagged and all the water collapsed the whole thing, so the boys started to dance in the pouring rain. We all had a ball and really started laughing. The wedding ceremony in Church was beautiful, lots of people came and the reception had a little excitement also. The wedding cake was brought in without the top. The lady that brought the cake in her van, had to stop suddenly (it happens in the traffic in Guatemala!) And the cake fell down! We had to fix it somehow, but it turned out real good anyway. I guess nobody noticed, I hope! We emptied all the living room and dining room for space and had rented tables and chairs for people to sit in. It was quite a crowd. I think all went well. The young couple went to Europe for their honeymoon! Eric and Sonia with little Danica, our first grandchild, came to the wedding from the States too. It was so good to see them.

So, our two boys are married, Eric married Sonia in the States and suddenly Walter and I are alone in the house. Maybe some of you know about the empty nest! But life goes on and as the years passed, we were privileged to see our grandchildren's firsts, in their dear lives. It did not last for long, but we are grateful for these times. I'll tell you later what happened.

A big loss 1985

Have you ever been afraid, worried, scared and perplexed all at the same time?   I was and it is not good! Remember I told you of my best friend Janet?   Her maid called one day, late afternoon and told me that the "lady" (that's what the maids called us) had a terrible headache, what she should do. Her husband was not home, he had gone to another little town. He was a missionary. I immediately drove to her house and yes, Jan was in a very bad shape. We hardly got her into the car to take her to her doctor. The Dr. came to the car to help me get Jan out, to take her to his office and then told me she should be hospitalized. Luckily the hospital is right next to his office. Then the hard time came for me. I had to read and sign I don't know how many papers! I felt like

I was signing Jan's death sentence. I was so nervous that most of what I read I did not know what it was.

Jan stayed at the hospital and I went to her house to spend the night with the children. Only the two little ones were at home, the three older ones were in the US already. One married, the other ones in college. So what did Jan have? A brain tumor! That was like a lightning bold hitting me. What to tell the children, where was John, the father? Finally John came and Jan was taken to the States for treatment. The young ones stayed with us. These are the times that you ask God, WHY? Heidi, the youngest, was only 12 years old. What a hard time for the family! Jan was operated on, had treatments, but died anyway. I never saw her again. Not even said good bye to her. Heidi stayed with us for a few years and then moved in with a family that had a girl Heidi's age, they went to the same school. I don't remember how long Tim stayed with us, but he went back to the States for college soon. I do not understand God's ways, but I do know that He knows best, He allows things for a purpose.

Families sometimes go through hard times and this was one of them for us. You think "these things will never happen to my family. "Divorce, No way! We don't do such things". Well, wrong again. Sonia left with the three children back to her Mama. What a hard thing it is to see your dear little innocent grandbabies go for good.

Eric had to stay in Guatemala because he went to college on a scholarship with the condition that he would work for the mission for 5 years, which he did.

We still had Danny and Susie, Gerhard's children, happy, lively Danny and Susie, the shy and sweet one. What a blessing they were, and still are! We love them and they sure filled our lives with joy.

I have to tell you of how God, in His special love and wisdom provides for us. He put Isabel in my life and what a friend she is to me! Now that Jan was gone, God knew that I needed a special friend like Isabel. What a blessing to have a friend like her. A friend that knows you, accepts who you are and gently invites you to grow and mature. "Isabel, you are a dear friend."

There are so many friends in our lives and we are thankful for all of them too. They all played a special part in our lives. But to mention them all would take another book! We just thank God for each one of them.

New horizons   1990

Here comes another surprise and gift from God!   Happy adventurous and loving Carol comes into our lives! How can I describe her? She is just a natural. You can count on her, to help and to tell you how it is!   Carol and Eric got married 1990. What a lot of fresh air came to our family!

Eric had a job to teach in Texas, so he left before Carol and she stayed with us for a time.   It was good and fun to have her with us. When she finally got her visa to go to the States, here goes Carol, not knowing a word of English, never been away from Guatemala and from her family. She is the oldest of 9 siblings. That takes a lot of guts! But, "US of America, here I come!"

Carol is not afraid of making mistakes, she spoke English as best she could and she made it in no time. I'm sure it was hard for her, but she is determined. Carol is a teacher now, but it took a lot of effort and jobs to get there. She cleaned houses, took care of old people, she continued with her studies and made it. God blessed Eric and Carol with two lovely and gifted children. Ludwig, a very loving personality and gifted Angie! "Here goes grandma", you will say. But I will tell you about our four grandchildren later.

Where do we come from?

People ask you here, in the States: "Where do you come from?" Where do I come from?? I was born in Dresden, Germany, grew up in Guatemala, Central

America and now live in beautiful St. Petersburg, Florida. I'll have to start from the very beginning. Don't worry. Not the VERY beginning! Pappy was born in Dresden, Germany and came to Guatemala as a young man for a big German coffee import and export firm. I remember that Mommy told me that it was the custom for all the young men from Germany that came to the city, to visit the German families to introduce themselves. So Pappy came to visit Mommy's parents the day my Mommy had her 15th Birthday. Here were all these silly girls, Mommy's girlfriends, all very curious about this young man, giggling and being silly. Pappy paid his visit, said good bye to the girls and left. The next morning he sent a bouquet of a dozen pink roses with a watch for Mommy as a Birthday present. Her parents said that she had to give the watch back. She could keep the roses, but had to give back the watch. Mommy was so embarrassed, she did not know how to give it back to him. Pappy took it very graciously and kept it for her, since he knew he was going to marry her sometime. Pappy had to wait till Mommy was 19 years old to marry her! Now on Mommy's side, Mommy's father came to Guatemala as a young man as a jeweler to a big jewelry store in Guatemala. He came from Hamburg, Germany. He married my Oma in Guatemala. So it goes with families!

Walter's father came to Guatemala as a young man at an invitation of his brother, who had already immigrated because of the depression in Germany. They had lived in the Black-forest in their father's farm, they were 9 siblings. Christian, Walter's uncle, started a farm in Guatemala. What a hard time he and his young wife must have had. No help and struggling with the weather, starting a farm and a family. They were real pioneers. They had 6 children. Walter's father bought a truck and started a transportation business. Walter's mother, what a courageous woman, came to Guatemala from Germany, as a young woman to marry this man who had asked her to come to Guatemala to marry him. She did not know what she was getting into!

Father had had a motorcycle accident, his leg was shattered. Mother did not know the language nor did she know anything about the culture. It must not have been easy for her, but, no complaints! They built their own little house and had two children, Walter and Inge. Mother helped with the finances with her baking. That's how our children remembered her "Oma's cookies".

So, that's where we come from and I still don't know, when asked where we come from: Germany, Guatemala, St. Petersburg, USA? I'll tell you later how I got to Guatemala.

Oh... who cares, all the epochs in our lives were so special and all led by a wise and loving God.

Life in Guatemala, now when I think back, I think: "how did we do all that?? " Walter was busy with his job as business manager for the mission of the Lutheran Church in Central America and Venezuela. Our budged was not so great either. We sure did cut back in our finances as he accepted the call to be the business manager of the Lutheran

Church in the Caribbean Area.

Walter had to travel a lot and I, busy with the children and all that was expected of me in the mission of the Church. Walter still had the time to build a little house on the big and beautiful lake Atitlan. A lake surrounded by mountains and three volcanoes. Indian villages were all around it. You have to see it to believe it, the beautiful colors of the Indian weavings. All they wear is hand woven and made, embroidered by them. What a wonder of color combinations! We still made time to enjoy the lake with our boys. Walter even bought an old boat. We all learned to water ski. I hope our boys will remember it as a special time in their lives. I know they were sorry when we had to sell the property. I still remember us picking up the children from school on Saturday noon. They had classes on Saturday mornings also. They went to a private school, the German School.

State schools in Guatemala are very inferior. So there are many private schools in Guatemala. We picked them up all packed with everything including the dogs, two dachsies, all ready for the week end and had a picnic on the way. Along we went through very curvy mountainous roads for three and a half hours, till we reached our destination, the beautiful Lake Atitlan. The town's name is Panajachel, another kaleidoscope of color and hustle with the Indians and their beautiful costumes trying to sell you anything they make or harvest. Beautiful hand woven material, jewelry, anything they make.

Unconditional love

I have to tell you about Dopey, our dachshund, he was born in our house a puppy among six brothers and sisters. He got his name from the seven dwarfs of Snow White. Dopey was always the last one to get to their mothers breast, if he made it at all. We had to push others away to give Dopey a chance. Dopey turned out not to be so Dopey. Once we were out on the boat, of course Dopey too. We were at a beach quite far away from where we have the house. Everybody is swimming, when we see that the south wind is coming. They call it "Chocomil" I think it means "South Wind" in the Indian language. That wind gets pretty strong! So, get everything from the beach, get the boys out of the water and off we go to the beach near our house. When we almost got to the house, "where is Dopey?" We left Dopey behind! Off goes Walter with the boat, puts the boat down the ramp and goes looking for Dopey.

He is nowhere to be seen! Calls him, looks all over, Dopey is not there. Can you imagine how we felt? When Walter comes back towards the house, here comes Dopey running! We still don't know how he got there. He must have swum some of the way, crossed fences, because some of the houses on the beaches are right by the water. It is still a riddle how Dopey found his way back!

Once we left Dopey at a lookout point. Again: "Where is Dopey?" We looked back and here comes Dopey running after us. He could have been run over by another car! Dopey is NOT so Dopey after all! Dear Dopey lived with us for 16 years. He even got competition later with another dacksie, Waldy. Waldy was a soccer player, all tough and playful. Sometimes he aggravated poor Dopey.

Don't tell me that dogs don't have personalities, they do! We had a series of dachsies in our married life and each one certainly had their own personality. Take Laila for instance, she was all lady and "don't you mess with me!" She became the mother of the seven dwarfs, Dopey's mother. No way did she let anybody but us, even look at her puppies. Then there was Putzie, he was a royal, all correct and don't bother me. Putzie had to put up with Waldy too, for a time. He did it with a lot of grace. Our last dacksie before we came to the States was another Waldy. He was all love and happiness! Waldy knew exactly when we went to the lake. He looked at Walter and if he had his jeans on, Waldy would not let him out of his sight. Waldy followed Walter all the time till the car door was opened and he jumped in. "Nobody takes me out of here" When we told him: : Do you want to come with us?" Waldy runs to get his blanket jumps into the car and ready to go! At the lake, he did not like the cold water, but when we threw him these stones that float, here Waldy had to dutifully retrieve it and place it at Walter's feet, all ready to go again. We had a hard time to leave Waldy behind, when we moved to the States! We left him with the nurse that worked with my brother Eric for so many years.

I think Waldy knew, because when Walter took him to Gloria's car, Waldy looked at him with such a sad expression. It was hard! I also have to tell you about Bobbie, Eric's dog. Wow, did he have a personality! I'll tell you about him later! I could go on and on with dog stories. When I grew up, we had a lot of dogs, those were all big dogs and some of them trained professionally.

Talking of animals, here comes Gerhard into the picture. Gerhard is an animal lover. When our children grew up, we had a variety of them! We had rabbits, baby squirrels, these we found in the garden hidden in a flower bed and we were afraid that the dogs would find them and harm them. So we took them in and nursed them till they were big enough to fend for themselves. We also had turtles, parakeets. One of them we caught in our garden, probably flew away from somewhere. He was a character! He would make somersaults when we told him to and all sorts of tricks to get our attention. We named him Panchito. Later, we had other Panchitos in our house. Believe it or not Gerhard even had a live tarantula in a box. He kept catching live flies for his "pet" until I gave him an alternative: either me, or the tarantula. One of us had to go. I'm glad he chose me and the tarantula had to go. He did not kill it! He took it to the ravine close to our house and let it go. I always thought Gerhard would become a Veterinarian, but no, he studied chemical engineering. Once, Gerhard and his cousin Laurie, my sister Rosie's daughter, nursed our mutt Robin back to health. He had Parvovirus a deadly sickness of dogs. The veterinarian had given him up.

Laurie and Gerhard spoon fed him day and night, chicken soup, for I don't remember how long and Robin survived and lived many more years. Robin, we found in the ravine near our house and the boys rescued him. He was just a puppy. He became a big dog, a funny looking one at that, but very loyal and loving. Robin had no tail and his front legs were shorter that the hind ones, so when he ran, it looked real funny!

So, that is the story of all our dogs, not really all of them. Rex was a German Shepherd, he made it his duty to take care of us when we went swimming. We had a hard time keeping him out of the swimming pool and since he was not able to get in, he ran around the pool and barked relentlessly, till we got out of the pool. Gerhard would throw a tennis ball for him to catch just to keep him quiet and that was pure pleasure for Rex. He was a beautiful dog and full of pep! I also told you about Teddy, the dog we had to rename when Jerry, Rosie's husband, came into our family. Teddy made it his business to keep all of us safe. A serious busyness for him! Teddy would not let anyone come into the garden or the house. I think he would bite anyone, although we never tried it, he was always put in his pen when somebody came, but he sure didn't like it when people got near to us. He would bark and be furious. But with us he was such a loving and playful dog. Teddy was poisoned by somebody, We were so sorry and sad when we found out.

Adventurous trip   1939

I haven't told you how I got to Guatemala. Remember I told you that I was born in Germany? Well, that was an adventure for poor Mommy. My parents had decided to take the children, that is my three siblings, to live in Germany for a time, since Pappy had a home in Dresden where my aunt, Tante Annie and our two cousins lived, taking care of Pappy's house.   So, off the whole family went although Pappy did not stay there all the time, because he still had the job in Guatemala. Fred and Rosie went to school there and Eric was still too young. Mommy was real surprised and not too happy when she found out that she was pregnant again! That was me.   That is

why I was born in Germany.   In 1939,
when there was a lot of talk about a war
and Hitler started to come into power
more and more, Pappy and Mommy
decided that we should all go back to
Guatemala.

Pappy flew ahead and Mommy, Oma and
us children were going to go back with the
big ship "The Caribia"   I still remember
the name!   Well all were on board, when
it was said that the ship might not be able
to go because of the war.   There was a
back and forth, the passengers were all in
arms and poor Mommy with 4 children
and Oma. What should she do? Many
passengers disembarked and wanted to
leave either by plane or who knows how
and Mommy stayed on board and
worried! After a time, it was decided that
the ship would go after all, so you can
imagine how relieved Mommy felt.   The
Caribia docked in Ellis Island, New York
and from there we took a plane to
Guatemala.   I'm sure Mommy was so
relieved to be able to get back and have
Pappy there to greet us.   So, here was
Mommy, left Guatemala with three
children and got back with four, without

anybody noticing it! Only later did we find out how much trouble that would be! I'll tell you later what that was.

Remember, I told you that Walter and I got married June 2nd, 1956? We had a wonderful wedding, just like Rosie and Jerry's. Pappy is good in organizing weddings and receptions. But here comes the trouble! We were planning on going to Europe for our honeymoon, so I had to get a passport. When we applied, I found out that I did not exist in Guatemala. I had a birth certificate from Germany, but nothing in Guatemala. So here I was, maybe even illegal. I could not get a passport from Germany because Dresden was in the Russian Zone! What to do??

Finally with a lot of back and forth and Pappy, relying on friends and connections, got the permission to add me into Walter's passport. That was not an easy task! It took us more than a month to get that taken care of. I even thought we were not going to be able to travel. So off we went on our honeymoon, after a really lovely wedding! We drove from Miami to New York to catch the plane to

Europe. I told you about the car we drove to New York. It was a fancy convertible car! On our way we heard the song on the radio "Que sera, sera", sung by Doris Day, so many times. It became our honeymoon song. "Que sera, sera, whatever will be, will be, the future is not ours to see, que sera, sera". Isn't it true in real life? You really don't know what the future will bring. It's good to know that we have a loving Father that knows.

A new world

More changes! Remember I told you that I did not like changes?
Who would have known that we leave Guatemala, our home, my parent's home and all our dear friends? Seems strange to me! Life in Guatemala wasn't safe any more, kidnapping, theft, violence. Our two boys left, Eric to the States, Gerhard to Canada, our grandchildren so far away. The decision was hard, but necessary. The selling of the properties was a miracle that only God could have

done: selling the big property of my parents and our house just at the right time. Talking about miracles! I could write a whole book of all the miracles in our lives!

Have you ever had your decisions all planned out without your knowing anything about it? That's what happened to us. It did take a lot of work and doing, but when we think back, we know that God had already planed it for us. We had a place to go to, we got our permanent residence visa of the States through our son Eric, everything just happened like it had to be, like our place here in Bay Island, St. Petersburg, with the most beautiful view on the water.

We had no intention of buying anything. We were in St. Petersburg FL on vacation. Just for fun, we contacted a Realtor, told him what we wanted and he showed us two apartments. They were nice, but that was it. The third one is the one we bought right then and there, the view did it to us, a huge window overlooking the bay. We had two weeks to get everything ready to be able to rent it out, luckily the apartment was furnished. Dear Karen, our "adopted" daughter helped us get everything in garage sales. I'll tell you about our dear Karen later. We sure rushed in getting the apartment ready to be able to rent it out, because I wanted to get back to Guatemala for the wedding of the son of my best friend Isabel. We made it! Back in Guatemala, we found out that the bride had gotten cold feet and there was not going to be a wedding! Surprise, surprise! Well it is good that they find out before they get married. We rented our apartment in St. Petersburg out for three years for the winter months, after that, we moved to the apartment, and everything was ready for us!

I have to tell you about our "daughter" Karen. What a blessing she is to us. God gave us a lovely and so loving daughter. We met her and her husband, John, in an apartment housing place, that we had rented to come on vacations before we bought our condo in Bay Island. We lived in the second floor and Karen and John in the first. We clicked right away and she still is such a blessing to us. When we bought the apartment in St. Petersburg, we had to get it ready to rent it out. That meant getting dishes, sheets etc. all the things for the apartment to be ready to live in. That's when Karen helped us so much, she took us to all the garage sales and estate sales in the area. We equipped the apartment completely in two weeks. Thank you Karen! Karen has become such an important part in or lives, not only because of all her help but because she is such a loving and happy person!

Do you like hurricanes? No? We don't either. So, for many years, we went to Henderson Bay in WA. To our dear friends Richard and Mimi's vacation house, in the summer. They are such good friends and were such a help and showed us so much love. We had many wonderful summers with them, trips to Hawaii and Mazatlan, Mexico. They always had the little house in Henderson Bay ready for us with the fridge full of goodies. What a lovely place, right on the bay, beautiful view on Mount Rainier covered with snow, The deer came to visit us, and the seals gave us the nicest show on the raft that was in the water. We will always be thankful to our dear friends, Richard and Mimi, for allowing us to enjoy this place for so many years.

I must say that the hurricanes have not touched St. Petersburg yet, but things can change. We still "run away" so to speak. There are times in our lives when God, in His great love, gives us signs in such a beautiful way. This has happened to us and I'm sure you have had similar experiences in your life and just marvel at His mercy and grace. This time I was so afraid that hurricane Wilma was coming our way to St. Petersburg. So here I look out the big picture window in our living room and I see a perfect rainbow from one side to the other. What a sight and what peace came unto me! Don't you tell me that God does not talk to you! He does in so many ways besides His Word, also in nature. When I see the marvels of His creation I want to sing "How great thou art, how great thou art"!
Hurricane Wilma never touched St. Petersburg.

What a job!!

Changes, changes, remember I don't like changes!   Well, there were so many changes in our life!   All for the better, when I look back on them, but at the time, they didn't look so good! First my parents die, a big change in our lives, suddenly I am the old one and all the family gatherings are up to us now. I sure appreciate all that Mommy and Pappy did for us, many happy remembrances. Now it is up to me!   I hope our children will   remember   their   childhood   and growing up with as much love as I did, when I grew up.   But then changes are a lot of work!   We had to empty my parent's big house because it was going to be rented out. What a job!   My parents were savers and had the room for it too. Where do you put all those things! The furniture was all so large. They don't construct houses that big any more, not in Guatemala. So we had an auction to sell them.   Dear Rosie, my sister and Jerry came to Guatemala to help us out. There were still a lot of things that we just gave away, some of the furniture Eric, my brother, took to his new home, a house he rented. But still so many things we just had to give away or throw away. I'm getting very experienced in emptying houses! Some years before, my dear Mother in Law passed away and we had to empty her house too, because we had to sell it. Was she a saver!! My goodness, her house was not that big, but she sure had a lot of stuff! We almost filled the garage with all the stuff we had to throw away! Can you imagine??

Then years later, it was Eric's, my brother's house that we had to empty. This was another real difficult thing to do for me because Eric passed away after a long struggle with cancer. We were with him the last year of his life and illness and it was sad and difficult for me! Eric and I were very close growing up.

Again, at Eric's house, what to do with all the books he had, all the furniture and dishes and most of all Bobbie, the big gray dog a Weimeraner. Bobbie was a friendly dog, but during Eric's illness, he was not allowed into the house because the nurses were afraid of him. So Bobbie did not like this treatment and barked and barked every time someone would come in. What to do with Bobbie? Finally we found out that this lady veterinarian was willing to take him. She came to the house and I was so afraid that Bobbie would harm her. The Vet gave us a pill to calm him down. "Just give him one" the Vet said. Nothing doing, Bobbie was so excited to be able to come into the house! He ran into every room. We gave him another pill. Bobbie was still all alive and running around. So the lady Vet told us to take him to her house later, when he calmed down. Bobbie never did calm down and we had the hardest time getting Bobbie into the car. Off we went, Bobbie barking and jumping around in the car. We delivered him and when we left, bark, bark from Bobbie! The next day I called the lady to see how things were, and no answer, I was so afraid that she was bringing Bobbie back to us. I did see her in Church and she told me: "Oh Bobbie is such a good dog and so obedient, we are so happy with him" Here went all my worries! "Thanks, Bobbie for cooperating!"

Now it was our house to empty! By this time I became a little careless and many things I just gave away, I had a garage sale also and the furniture just stayed in the house. Our house at the lake got the same treatment. I really just took things that I really cherish with us.

So, talking about changes, everything sold! The four houses, my parents' big house, ours, Eric's and the house at the lake. All gone! A funny feeling! But, life goes on... I guess!

USA, here we come   2004

Life DOES go on! We moved to beautiful St. Petersburg right to our apartment all ready for us! I did tell you how we got that apartment. God knew already that we would need a place to stay! We love it there and He even provided dear friends and a loving daughter, our dear Karen. I already told you about Karen and all the help she was to us to get the apartment ready for the time we wanted to rent it out. Our dear friends, Dorle and Claus live just two doors away from us and what a big help they are to us, truly good friends. We sure appreciate their friendship! Thank you, God!

Then we also met Hilde and Ernie, both from Europe, Hilde from Germany and Ernie from Austria who now live in Canada and come down to Florida during the winter months. Such good friends and Hilde, always ready to help in anything she can.

Talking about God providing, remember that I told you that during the summer months we went to Henderson Bay at our dear friend's summer house? We were always welcomed by them and they helped in so many ways.

After so many years of enjoying the beautiful scenery there, it was time to move on (talking about changes!) We noticed that it was getting to be a burden for our friends Mimi and Richard, us coming every year. We get older and they did so much for us, we will always be thankful to them, but sometimes it does get too much. So here, God provides again! We met our dear and special friends in Henderson Bay. Lee and Fran, what a lovely and friendly couple! Lee says he collects people, he sure does! We became close friends and when they sold their house in Henderson Bay, we were sad, but here they call us and say: "Come here to Birch Bay, Blaine in Washington State, it is beautiful here!" So there we went without having a clue how it would be, pure faith in our friends! It was worth it!

2006
Birch Bay, in Blaine is real close to the Canadian border, close to Vancouver, where our Gerhard and his family live.

Our friends had a Real Estate lady ready for us and can you imagine! We fell in love with the third house she showed us and bought it. This was shortly before we went on a cruise to Alaska to celebrate our 50th Wedding Anniversary with our children and grandchildren. What a fun time we had with them! I'll tell you all about our friends Lee and Fran later, when I introduce them to you! What a blessing they are! Thank you Lord for them!

Now we have to furnish the house in Birch Bay. No idea where to go what to do. We just bought the beds, living room (not all of it) and dinning room. The rest was the help and kindness of our friends, Lee and Fran and also from Richard and Mimi. The dear ones donated a lot of things. Garage sales were also visited and ... here we are in a completely furnished house. Talking of God providing!

Now we have two houses, one in Washington for summer and an apartment in Florida for winter! How long we will be able to go back and forth? Only God knows. For right now, we are enjoying the beauty of WA and the beaches in Florida. There are no beaches like in Florida, each place with its own special beauty.

Guatemala

Talking about places we have lived. People ask me what I liked most about Guatemala. Memories, memories, some good and others not so good, but thinking of the country in itself, the beautiful scenery! Guatemala is a small country, the whole country much smaller than a State of Texas. Surrounded by mountains and volcanoes, 27 of them, and I don't mean little ones. Three of them are still active, you can see them when they erupt, just like fireworks.

They throw ashes and sand too, sometimes to the city and many times we had to run to bring the cloths in because we dried them outside in the sun. Our dear friend from Germany once told us, when she was vacationing in our little house at the lake, "wait till I write to my family that here in Guatemala we have to shovel ashes and sand, instead of snow"

I loved the Indian people. They have their own culture, dress code and values. Talking of values, they sure respect their elders and they take care of them. Their clothes are hand woven and embroidered. What a canopy of color. They can combine colors in a wonderful way. Each village has its own dress code.

Each bigger village has its own market day and what a sight that is. All the people of the surrounding villages come and they carry all the things they want to sell, the men on their backs and the women on their heads. It is quite a sight to see. Market day is very important to them, maybe only their one social get together. It is really beautiful to see. Then there is Lake Atitlan surrounded by mountains and three volcanoes sticking out in all their majesty, a big beautiful lake. I already told you about this lake. We spent many a weekend and vacation time there with our children. I told you about Walter constructing a little house there just with an Indian Mason. What a nice man he was. We have many special memories of that place. It is also a tourist attraction. Talking of tourist attraction, there is the town of Antigua, with all the big ruins of the churches that were destroyed in a big earth quake.

The Spaniards sure built a lot of churches, not only there, but in every little village. The beautiful carpets they do out of saw dust of many colors right on the streets during Holy Week, when they have their big processions of Jesus carrying his cross. They carry these big figures all around town. There is a lot to see in Guatemala, just get a brochure and you will see a lot! I also liked the vegetation, so different in each area. The vegetation in the highland is completely different from the one in the coast. You can drive from one coast to the other in five hours from the Pacific Ocean to the Atlantic Ocean.   Guatemala City is a mile high city, you drive down to the ocean, to sea level in two hours. If you want to see something beautiful, don't go to the city, go to the countryside.   The city is overrun by people. Three million in one small place!

Then there is Lake Amatitlan, a smaller lake and closer to the city. We went there a lot too. Now it is completely polluted, such a shame. It used to be such a nice lake. We would go there with my parents, when I grew up.   I told you about that too. Then, when we had our children and they were older, we bought a house there by the lake and also had so many nice weekends   there.   So   many   Birthday parties we celebrated there with our friends and family. For every Birthday there had to be a piniata of course. So...now I told you what I liked most! I still miss our many friends. God blessed us with many truly good friends there.

The beauty of friendship

I told you that I would introduce you to our friends in, first in Henderson Bay and then in Birch Bay, where we landed after saying good bye to Henderson Bay and our dear friends Richard, Mimi and our dear Kristin, their daughter. It's not really good bye, it's "Auf Wiedersehen" Till we see you again. Seattle, where they live, is not so far away from Blaine, where we are now. We can still see each other! Meet Lee and Fran! Lee says he is a people collector and he sure is! At our daily walks in the morning in Henderson Bay, here comes a man... We greet each other: "Good morning" talk a little bit and we are hooked! The next day, while we were picking wild blackberries on our way, here we hear Lee: "Hey, do you want real nice ones and other fruits too?" Of course we wanted. So he took us to his house, introduced us to Fran, his wife and off we went with fruits as much as we could carry. We were invited many times to delicious dinners at their house and they came to our house also. A wonderful friendship started.

Lee came over to pick clams with our children and grandchildren while they were there visiting us. He showed them how to open them. Came with his power cleaner to clean the patio, helped wash the windows. Lee is something else!

Changes again!

I told you about Lee and Fran selling their house in Henderson Bay and moving to Birch Bay in the State of Washington. That's why we landed in Birch Bay! They invited us to visit them and when we arrived, they had a Realtor and all we needed to buy a house. And what did we do? We bought a house! I told you already when we bought the house. What a beautiful area. The bay is so beautiful, the forest with all the huge Cedars and other pine trees. Birds, deer, raccoons, squirrels and they say coyotes, which we have never seen at all. And best of all: We are real close to the Canadian border and can visit with Gerhard and family who live in Vancouver! And here I am the person that doesn't like changes! We even found a Church, Grace Lutheran Church right close, in Blaine! Now, if that isn't our loving God working in our lives again!

We go to Birch Bay in the summers. Before we knew it, we had real good neighbors and dear friends in the area, besides Lee and Fran who really are like family to us! The house we bought for our 50th Anniversary! The Lord has blessed us and we are very thankful!! So here we are!

The gift of music

You know, when you live with something, you take it sooo for granted. I want to tell you about Walter and the gift of music that he has and the marvel of it is, that it has passed on to the other generation. I don't mean the ability to be able to play an instrument when you learn it, I mean playing an instrument without having had an opportunity to learn it. Walter plays the organ, piano, accordion, trumpet and the violin well, I don't mean playing the little melody, but playing it well with accompaniment and all. He played the organ for our Church in Guatemala for many years and started a brass choir. Our boys played with the brass choir also. He played the accordion at our youth gatherings, directed the Church choir and so on.

I remember Walter telling me that he learned to play the trumpet when he joined the brass choir in Germany. The ability to play an instrument just like that, was passed on to the next generation This is the case with, Daniel, our grandson, Gerhard's son and also Angie, our granddaughter, Eric's daughter. What a joy it is to hear them play. You are going to think: "Here comes the grandmother" but it really is so. When Danny was in High School at the German school in Guatemala, Danny was always asked to play the piano when important dignitaries came to the school. He just sat down and played well. He also played for his graduation. Danny still plays for his Church and their missions. Danny has the advantage also that he took classes in playing the piano besides playing just like that!

Angie has an incredible gift with the violin and specially her voice! What a beautiful voice she has! She was accepted at the State choir of Kansas, her being only a sophomore in High School. The choir is going to Europe on a concert tour. By the way, Eric also has a very good voice. Am I bragging too much? I'll tell you a little story. When Eric and Gerhard were in High School, this is in the German school in Guatemala, there was going to be a musical in school. Eric just told us that we could come, if we wanted to. I even considered if I should go or not. Well, I decided to go and when I got to school I was greeted there with the question, "are you Eric's mother? He is the solo voice in the musical, what a good job he does!" Eric never told us! He does have a good voice and he still has.

I could go on and on about our children

and grandchildren, but... NO, I can't do that. I remember grandparents get into doing that: telling all about these wonderful kids, all straight "A" students, tall and gifted and I told myself I would never do that! I hope I didn't over do it. So coming back to GIFTS, they are all from God. Everybody has a special gift that God gave him or her! I told you about Danny and Angie's gift of music. I think of Susie, Gerhard's daughter, such a loving heart, always ready to help and care besides being so good in the University. She just graduated from the University of British Columbia with a degree of Biochemist. Then we have Ludwig such a friendly and caring person, he graduated from High School May 2009.

Now I wonder what my gift is. I love children, I love to teach and I love old folks and I love people, so maybe there is my gift. But I will tell you what I don't have! NO sense of direction. Here I am in a place and I have no inkling where I am! That makes it a challenge. Two new places to find my way: Florida and Washington. In Guatemala I could at least drive to the familiar places I had to go, but now?? I even have to pay real good attention when I go to the rest room in the airport to find my way back to where we were sitting. Even when we go into another door at the grocery store, I am all confused! Am I glad that I have Walter! That reminds me of an adventure I had with Eric, he was only 8 years old! We came back from Germany and had a layover in Miami, so we stayed overnight in a Motel. Walter and Gerhard were sick with the Flu and I wanted to go shopping into town. So Eric and I took the bus and off we went! We walked to this big Mall and wandered around looking at every thing, I made sure I looked where we came into the store and where the bus stop was when we came in. So it was time to go back to the Motel. When we came out, I was lost! Where were we? Where is the bus stop? Erich said:" Mami we came out from another door, this is not the door we came into! Trouble, trouble, I had no idea what to do. So young Eric guided me to the right place to where we could take the bus back to the Motel. No kidding, if I would have been alone, who knows where I would have landed. Those are my challenges. Believe me, they are no fun!

Walter takes care of the finances. Thank God for that! He is so good at that. I am the cook and social director. I love the last one the most!

God's unending blessings

People have asked me how I like it living in the States. I LOVE it! There are so many things I like here. The cleanliness, the service people give. Everything is well organized. You know, when people begin to complain about the States, Walter and I just look at each other and try to smile at the people. If they only knew! We tell each other that we will send them to live in another third world country for three months. Believe me, they will come back very thankful for where they live. In Florida we live in a community of people 55 years and over and we have seen some complainers! I wish they would appreciate of what they have!
But then I am very happy that I grew up

and lived in a place where everything is not all that perfect and everything can be a challenge in so many ways.

The Latin culture is completely different and especially in Guatemala where there are a mixture of cultures, the Ladinos, the Indians and the mixture of them. I admire the Indians. They are hard working people, especially agriculture on very rugged land. Their family is very important to them. Older people are respected and obeyed. Now the Ladinos, a mixture of Spanish and Indian, don't take honesty or work so seriously, lying is part of life for them. Then there are the "pure" Spaniards and other foreign cultures that mostly keep to them selves. Growing up in Guatemala, we had very good friends in all the different cultures. Guatemalans are friendly people. I do miss our friends there!

Now about being happy to have lived in a country and culture that is not that well organized, and not everything works that well, I'll give you only some examples, the water supply. In the time of our marriage and with the children, water came only a few hours in the day. We collected the water in some water containers, but we had to be careful of not using water too much or the supply would not last for when we needed it! You learn to save!! We never watered the lawn. It turned brown in the dry season and got real nice and green in the rainy season. Then there were electricity outages. No electricity, no water, no light, candles were always handy, so were the matches. But we all took these things in stride, that's the way life was. I remember going to the grocery store and praying that there would be a parking space. There is not enough space for many parking places in each store.

Getting your license plate or sticker for the car, you had to stay in line for a LONG time and then, when you finally got to the window, we were told that this was not the right window, it is that other one on the left. So, we waited at the other window a long time. If you were lucky, you got to the right place in time, before they closed for the lunch hour. For any official document, you'd better take your time.
But then the way people just took any challenge gracefully and happily, that's

the way things are! No problem. While helping out in the mission in Church, I had to do with a lot of poor people. They take things as they come, they are happy people. The children grow up making their own toys. They are happy children. Of course there are the exceptions, there are criminals also. But that is all over the world.

I keep thinking of the book I once read: "Small is beautiful". I lost that book, it was so good!

Guatemalans are very family minded. I learned to love and admire these people, they became good friends and I learned many things from them!

The old people always live with their family. They take care of each other. There is great respect for the older generation. Indians are hard working people. Guatemala being so mountainous, there are no roads they walk to their fields, carry their things on their backs. Market days are in different villages and they all walk there carrying their goods, the men on their backs, the women on their head. No bad posture for these women!

So, having grown up in a different culture, opens up your eyes for so many things and we appreciate what we have, now much more.

Now, the weather in Guatemala, I can't complain about the weather, "The land of eternal spring" that's what they call Guatemala and that is true. There are only Rainy Season and Dry Season. In the Dry Season everything turns brown, in the Rainy Season everything turns green. Grass, plants and all the vegetation is lush and green.

That is the way it was in our garden too, because we never watered the garden, only the flower beds, if it was really necessary. Remember I told you about the water supply! So, when you have lived in a place where everything is not taken for granted, you learn to be appreciative of what you have now. Always, running water, people come on time, when they say they will, service is of a matter of course, the streets are clean, no fences around the houses. In Guatemala City all houses are fenced in, big walls, many with barbed wire on top. The stores in Guatemala City all have a guard with a machine gun in their hand at the entrance. The little stores have iron bars before the counters. So many people, especially children are begging in the streets. So I tell everybody that wants to hear me "Appreciate what you have". People here in the States, do take so many things for granted, especially young people do.

How about protection? I have to tell you a story about God's protection in so many ways. I know the Lord protects us every day, but in these peculiar ways, it is really worth telling you about it. I used to go to the cemetery in Guatemala to take flowers to my parent's grave, there is where our little ones are buried also. So when I went, Tura always insisted on going with me. Tura stayed with us, first with my parents, then with Walter and me until he died. What a faithful servant! When he accompanied me to the cemetery, he always had something in his hand wrapped in newspaper. I finally found out that it was his "machete" a big bush knife that the Indians use for everything, I guess protection too. Tura wanted to go with me to protect me! So here I go always the same routine: out of the car to buy flowers in the little flower market, back to the car on my side, put the flowers on the back seat and into the car, the driver's side. Only this time, I don't know why, the only explanation I have is: God's protection, I come out of the market, go to the other side, put the flowers in the trunk , one thing I never did , go around the other side to my side, the drivers side and into the car. I did notice that there was a man on my side by the door, when he saw me go the other way, he followed me, but by the time he got to me I was in the car with the door locked and the window closed, like we always drive in the city, he tries to talk to me, but I did not pay any attention to him and started the car. Tura was all pale and I asked him what was the matter and he just pointed to the man, it was then that I saw that he had a big knife in his hand and was pointing it to me. I thanked the Lord for His protection. How many times we are protected and don't even know it! Like keeping me healthy even though at the mission in Guatemala I was with people with leprosy, with HIV, whooping cough and I never thought anything about it. Now I do! My family could have been affected by this too!

Another adventure with God's protection: I was riding in the bus in Guatemala City, I often did this to avoid driving in the heavy traffic. There was a seat in the middle of the bus, so there I sat. The bus was pretty full, like they always are and here two men standing in the back started arguing, out come their pistols. They started shooting! The driver stops the bus and everybody jumps out of the bus, there are two doors, one in the back the other in the front. I was so startled that I just sat there. I don't even know if someone got hurt or not. The bus got empty in a hurry, except for me and the driver. The driver closes the doors and off we went, the driver and me. I was so shocked that I was not able to move, but got home safe and sound, with a little quiver in my legs. Yes, life is different in other countries.

Life changes with time as the cities get bigger and more people live in one place. That is what happened in Guatemala, specially in the city, since many of the rural people come to the city thinking they will get a better life and work there, which is absolutely not so. There is no work, the city grows bigger and no room, not enough water supply, especially in a place that is so small because it is surrounded by mountains and volcanoes. All these problems were not the case when we grew up in the city. This came later.

I have to laugh, because when Walter built our house in the city, he did it with a really wonderful person, a very simple mason. We did have to have a building permit to build the house. While we were waiting for the permit, the mason said: "Let's start building anyway." So we did, our boys even helped hauling the cement in a little cart. Walter did all the pluming and electricity work. Our mason, Don Chente, was his name, had his helpers. The house was built, we lived in it for 29 years, we sold the house and we are still waiting for the building permit! That's life in Guatemala, I guess! You learn to take things as they are and live with it. There are no roadside rest areas in Guatemala. When we drove to the big lake, 3 ½ hours away from the city, the boys had to go to the bathroom many times. So we stop the car by the roadside and they go in the bushes, hoping they will not step on a snake. No problem. I went sometimes too! No restroom facilities in the parks either. The men go by a tree, the ladies are more modest.

Before we had the little house at the big lake, we would go camp in a tent. It never came to our minds to go to a hotel. You just make do with what you have. I don't know if I want to do it now! You get used to commodities in a hurry!

Am I getting old? Sometimes Rosie, my very dear sister, and I do reminiscence about our childhood and what a protected and orderly life we had. The huge house with all the servants at first, the big garden, swimming pool and tennis court and the so many really good times we had... our singing at night when we walked to the "new road" as we called it, watching the sky full of stars. The very special time we had at Christmas. Presents were never the most important part, it was the preparation, the music, the excitement, also the going to Church. The games we played. No television at that time!

We had to put our things away where they belonged, remember when we had the drilling every Saturday? When we failed to put our bicycles away, they were confiscated for a time. No bikes for a long time! We learned fast not to forget. Life with the children now is so different, when I see all the toys and bikes lying around now, I wonder if these kids are not missing something very important. To appreciate what they have and be responsible. So now I really sound like an old lady!

Working for the mission 1961/93

Another thing that I remember when we lived in Guatemala, as our boys were growing up and Walter worked with the Lutheran mission. His job was to supervise the Missions in Mexico, Guatemala, Honduras, El Salvador, Nicaragua, Costa Rica, Panama and Venezuela. Walter had to be away often, which was not very easy for me. We had many visitors from the States staying with us, usually missionaries or dignitaries of the Church. I guess the Schieber house was the place to stay, everybody thought. We met all sorts of people. I remember dear Florence and her husband Bob. Every time we would drive somewhere to show them the sights, Bob would exclaim with a sigh of relief: "Thanks be to God we are home!" when he saw the street that would lead us to our house. The traffic in the city really did it to him! You have to get used to the crazy traffic in the city! I also went to the hospital with the missionary wives, when the babies were born. Many times the husbands were at the "field" too far to come back in time. I remember when once dear Marilyn was already in the delivery room when her husband came rushing in and wanted to go into the delivery room to be with his wife. He was a big strong man! In he went! Not too long later, out he came again as white as a sheet! I was really worried that he would faint, so I told him to sit there on the floor by the door of the delivery room and I sat beside him. We waited there till the nurse came out and told us that he had a beautiful baby girl! We survived that one!

I love to share each story with you in a person's life. It is so full of God's grace and leading!

St. Petersburg and Birch Bay

Now I will "jump" back to St. Petersburg. One thing I am so thankful for, besides our dear friends Dorle and Claus, is the ladies Bible Study group that Dorle took me to. What loving and friendly ladies I met there. They accepted me with all their love and made me feel so welcome. I miss them when we are in Birch Bay, WA. I want to describe them to you without mentioning their names. Maybe you, ladies, will recognize each other and have some fun with this. This is the way I see you. First of all, they all love the Lord Jesus and really show it!

So here it goes: There is a very wise and loving lady. I admire her wisdom in so many ways. She has the gift of making everybody feel included. Then there is the straight forward one, she tells us how it is and that is that. She is a lot of fun and also very caring. Then there is the worrier, how I love her! She has a heart of GOLD. Always ready to help or do something for you. Then there is the outgoing one all full of enthusiasm for the Lord and for everything. She is sooo blessed. She is a lot of fun. Then there is the loving one, I mean really LOVING, caring and always happy to help. She is a blessing for many! Another dear one I love, she is so positive and happy, although she has had sad things happen in her life, what a good example she is to me. We also have the intellectual one, she loves her dictionary and always has something very good to share. I admire her. Then there is the inquisitive one, she wants to learn so much and does not even know how much wisdom she has and shares. What a lovely lady. One more I want to mention is this dear lady that is a miracle for me! God kept her here for a very good reason. I thank the Lord for her. Ladies, there are more of you, but I don't want to make this too long for the others! I just hope you had fun seeing how I see you and how much I have learned from you! I am so thankful for each one of you! I also wonder at God's love and wisdom, putting these special and so different "flowers' in one wonderful bouquet and all members of the Body of Christ!

Precious moments

I want to tell you about more recent "Highlights" in our family! This is 2008. How our grandchildren grow so fast! Our dear Daniel got married to a wonderful girl in Vancouver. Tara is so special to us and it is a joy to welcome her as our granddaughter. We were so happy to be able to be there for their wedding. They had a lovely wedding, all planed by them. Gerhard and Roxy, Danny's parents, had the rehearsal dinner for them at their home and Judith, Tara's mother, had us over to her house also, to meet the family. We were so thankful that we were able to be with them at such a special occasion.

Another special occasion in our lives! This is 2009 already! Susie graduated from the University of British Columbia in Bio Chemistry, Ludwig graduated from High School and Angie is a junior in High School already! Where did time go?? We are married for 53 years!
People have asked us "what do you do, to stay married for so long". Our advice is: LOVE, commitment, forgiveness and pray TOGETHER every day. There are ups and downs in every marriage, but sticking it out together is really worthwhile. We have a history together, that is more than many couples can say. I thank God for our marriage I know He brought us together.

Conclusion

Now that we are older, we think more

about death and what we still have to go through, will we be sick or have dementia? We also think about eternal life. This is something we can be sure of, isn't that wonderful to know? We already know that Jesus died for us; he carried all our sins on His shoulder unto the cross, so that we can be assured of our salvation and eternal life with our loving God. "For God so loved the world that He gave his only begotten Son, that whosoever believes in Him will not perish but have everlasting life". *John 3:16*

I have to tell you that I did not believe this at one time of my life. Remember when I told you about loosing our little ones in the accident?
I went through the faces of: Why my children, when there are so many children in the streets? So many WHYS! But another thing that got into my confused mind was: What if there is no Eternal life, no life after death? Maybe it is just a saying to comfort people that are grieving. Well, God took care of that in His wonderful way. Don't tell me that God does not talk to you! He does! Every time I opened the Bible at random,

here was His Word in John 14: 1-7.. "Let not your heart be troubled, believe in God and also believe in me. In my Father's house there are many mansions; if it were not so, I would have told you. I go to prepare a place for you. And if I go to prepare a place for you, I will come again and receive you to myself, that where I am there you will be also. Where I go you know (eternal life in heaven with Him) you know the way. Thomas said to Him: Lord, we don't know where you are going, how can we know the way? Jesus said to him: "I am the way, the truth and the life. No one comes to the Father except through me." Our heavenly Father kept repeating and repeating this verse for me in Church, in Bible reading, Bible studies, at funerals, it was just incredible! He still does, not as often as in those days, but often enough to get that through to this doubting child of His. I tell you this, so that you too may not doubt, but thank the Lord. He sure was patient with me!

So when Walter and I wonder about our future, we can sing our honeymoon song, with a happy heart: "Que sera, sera, whatever will be, will be, our future is not ours to see, que sera, sera" We don't know what our future will be, but our God does!! We thank our loving God!! We trust HIM and HIS unending LOVE and GRACE.

I dedicate this book to Walter, my husband, my lover, my friend and my helper.

114

Table of contents

Made in the USA
Coppell, TX
04 February 2025

45409246R00066